JOHN CORIGLIANO

STOMP

FOR SCORDATURA VIOLIN

ED 4654
First Printing: April 2017

ISBN: 978-1-4950-6492-0

G. SCHIRMER, Inc.

DISTRIBUTED BY
 HAL•LEONARD®
7777 W. BLUEMOUND RD. P.O. BOX 13819 MILWAUKEE, WI 53213

halleonard.com
musicsalesclassical.com

STOMP was commissioned for the XIV International Tchaikovsky Competition
St. Petersburg, Russia

The Competition Prize for Best Performance of the Commissioned Work
was awarded to Nigel Armstrong (USA)

Composer's Note:

When considering the type of piece to be written for a competition in 2011, I felt an impulse to wander from the expected. Rather than compose a virtuoso étude or a lyrical essay (as the judges would have dozens of pieces demonstrating those virtues), I envisioned a more interesting piece that would test a performer's imagination, intelligence and musicality by offering non-traditional problems to solve.

Hence, this unaccompanied six-minute study I call *STOMP*.

STOMP provides aural, artistic and physical challenges to the player. First, the violin's two outer strings are tuned to non-standard pitches. The mis-tuning (scordatura) deepens the instrument's range and replaces the usual perfect fifths between strings with grating dissonances. The player's ear is forced to hear pitches not usually heard from their instrument, as well as play pitches on a different string and position altogether. Second, the piece is modeled not on classical precedents, but on American fiddle music — bluegrass and jazz. And third, as in fiddle playing, the violinist must periodically stomp with his or her foot along with the music, testing their coordination and extending the physicality of "normal" violin playing.

For the Tchaikovsky Competition, the contestants were only provided with music printed at sounding pitch. Each violinist was set to task to determine which strings and fingerings would produce the intended result on their mis-tuned instruments. In addition to the original version, this edition contains a part realized and edited by Lara St. John for whom the piece is dedicated. This part is notated as it would be played to produce the intended result.

STOMP demands a theatrical mind, an unerring ear, and a delight in making music with the entire body. It is supposed to be fun for the audience and a workout for the violinist.

—John Corigliano

Duration ca. 6 minutes

Information on John Corigliano and his works is available at:
musicsalesclassical.com
johncorigliano.com

for Lara St. John
STOMP

John Corigliano (2010)
*Scordatura Violin part
by Lara St. John*

* *The Scordatura Violin part is an edited and realized version of the original composition which was written at sounding pitch, and shown above.*

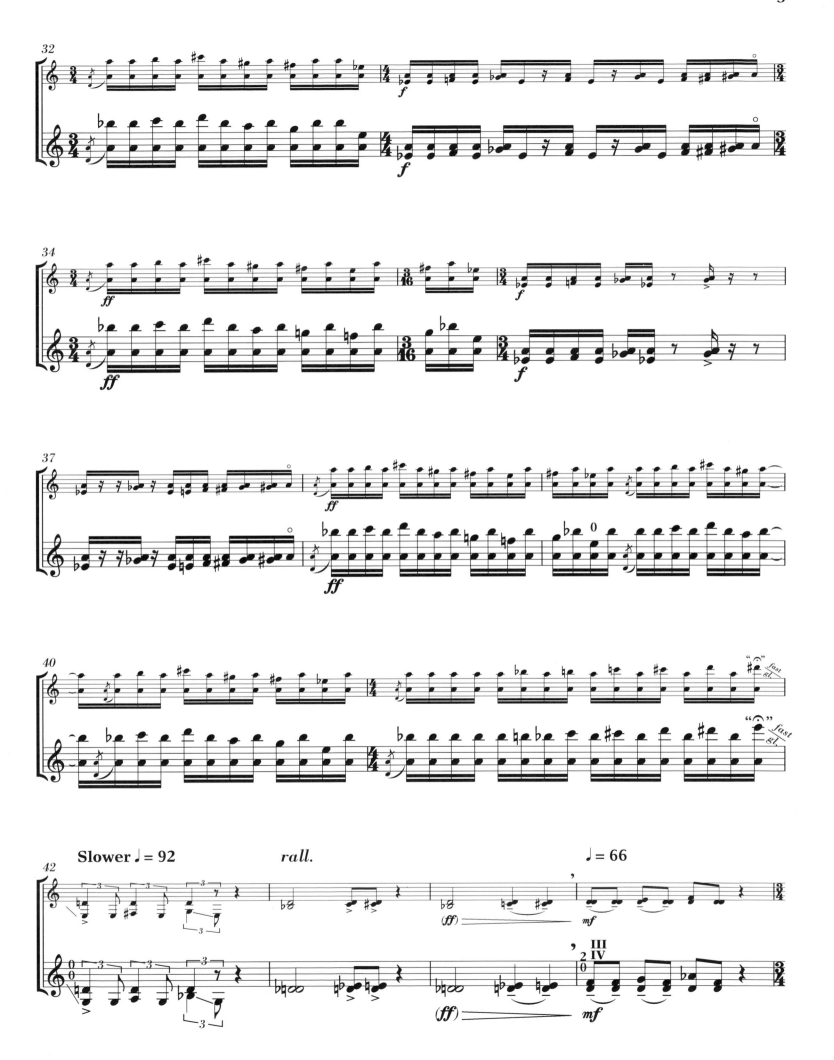

* "Crunch": Lightly mute the indicated strings with your hand in first position. Bow with *extreme* pressure, "al tallone," using a short bow stroke. Do *not* take the bow off the strings. The result should be a loud scratchy sound with no discernable pitch.

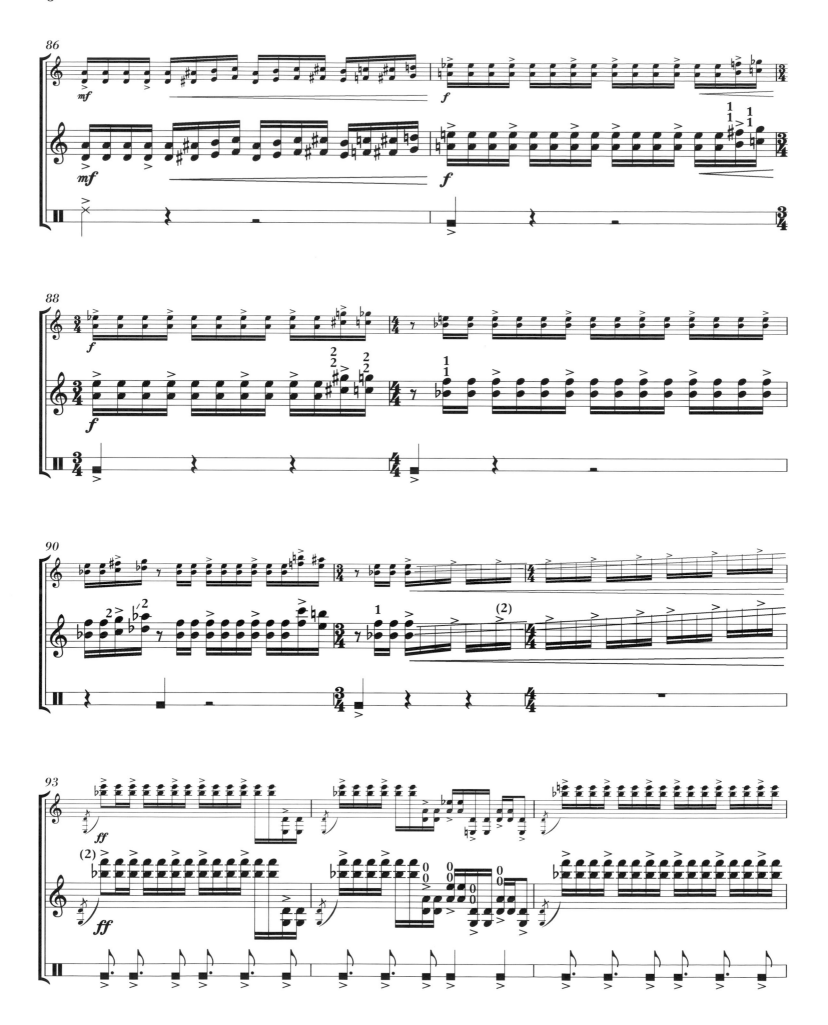

Slower ♩ = 92

♩ = 84

Slower ♩ = 72 *molto rall.*

mark upper voice melody

mark upper voice melody

A tempo primo (♩ = ca. 120–132)